Who Are
Suni and Butch?

Who Are Suni and Butch?

by Kirsten Anderson

illustrated by Dede Putra

Penguin Workshop

PENGUIN WORKSHOP
An imprint of Penguin Random House LLC
1745 Broadway, New York, NY 10019
penguinrandomhouse.com

Library of Congress Cataloging-in-Publication Data is available.

First published in the United States of America by Penguin Workshop, 2025

Manufactured in the United States of America
CJKW

ISBN 9798217244744 (paperback)
10 9 8 7 6 5 4 3 2 1

ISBN 9798217244751 (library binding)
10 9 8 7 6 5 4 3 2 1

The authorized representative in the EU for product safety and compliance
is Penguin Random House Ireland, Morrison Chambers, 32 Nassau Street,
Dublin D02 YH68, Ireland, https://eu-contact.penguin.ie.

Contents

Who Are Suni and Butch?

Late in the afternoon on March 18, 2025, the dolphins had come out to play. It was a perfect day, not too warm and not too cool. The blue skies were streaked with just a few thin clouds, and the water was calm, with only gentle swells rolling across its surface.

The dolphins leaped over the soft waves in the waters off the coast of Tallahassee, Florida, with no boat traffic to interrupt their play.

Suddenly, a giant object splashed down into the sea, shattering the peaceful silence. The dolphins scattered, but then, as the waters calmed, the curious animals began to approach. They skipped around, investigating the newcomer.

It wasn't a sea creature, though, or even a boat. The mysterious silver thing bobbing in the water was the SpaceX Dragon capsule *Freedom*, and it was bringing the members of Crew-9 back to Earth.

The safe return of any astronaut crew is always a happy event. But this one included two unusually famous astronauts: Suni Williams and Butch Wilmore. They had traveled to the International Space Station (ISS) in early June 2024, expecting to return to Earth a few days later. But plans can change in space, and their return was delayed— by almost three hundred days!

During their long stay in space, millions of people on Earth became fascinated by their story.

Now the world watched as the capsule was towed onto a recovery boat—with its dolphin friends following. At last, the crew emerged, smiling and waving.

Few people get to fly into space. But many could still relate to this particular story. Travelers often experience moments when their plans go off schedule. A flight is delayed or canceled. A car gets stuck in traffic. Connections are missed. People often get angry when their plans go wrong. But what do you do when a trip that was supposed to last a week turns into a nine-month stay . . . in space?

For brave astronauts like Suni Williams and Butch Wilmore, the unexpected is just part of the job.

Who are Suni and Butch? And how did they get through their extra-long space adventure?

CHAPTER 1
Suni

Sunita "Suni" Pandya was born on September 19, 1965, in Euclid, Ohio, to Dr. Deepak Pandya, a neuroanatomist, and Bonnie Pandya, an X-ray technician. When Suni was about a year old, the family, including Suni's older brother, Jay, and sister, Dina, moved to Needham, Massachusetts, for her father's work.

Suni was always very active. She took swimming and horseback riding lessons when she was very young and later began to swim competitively. Suni started running as part of her swim team training and found she enjoyed that, too. At age seventeen, Suni was too young to officially enter the Boston Marathon, but she decided to run it just for fun. Near the halfway point, her shoes began to feel uncomfortable, so she took them off. Suni ran the last twelve miles barefoot!

Suni in high school

Suni loved animals and originally planned to become a veterinarian. When it came time for Suni to choose colleges, her brother, Jay, was attending the US Naval Academy in Maryland. He thought that Suni would enjoy it there, too. Suni liked that idea and followed him to Maryland.

At the Naval Academy, Suni studied physical sciences. After she saw *Top Gun*, a movie about navy fighter pilots, she decided she wanted to explore the skies.

After graduating from the Naval Academy in 1987, Suni passed the requirements to become a Basic Diving Officer. She hoped to go to flight school to become a jet pilot, but there weren't any openings. Instead, she trained as a helicopter pilot. Suni flew support missions for Operation Desert Shield and for other operations in the Mediterranean and Middle East. She also was part of a crew that provided support for devastated Florida communities after the very destructive Hurricane Andrew in 1992.

In January 1993, Suni entered the US Naval Test Pilot School. During a visit to the Johnson Space Center in Houston, Suni's class heard retired astronaut John Young speak. Young explained that he and other astronauts had learned how to fly helicopters as a way to practice the moon landing. Suni realized that her skill as a helicopter pilot might make her a good candidate for spaceflight.

After graduating from test pilot school, Suni worked on testing many different types of helicopters. She also became an instructor at the school. But she still was thinking about space, and she applied to become an astronaut.

Suni's application was rejected. She wasn't very surprised. Many qualified people applied for the astronaut program and few were accepted. One of her squadron commanders had even said that she didn't have a chance because the program preferred jet pilots over helicopter pilots.

Suni didn't give up. She knew more education would help her chances, so she got a master's degree in engineering management from the Florida Institute of Technology in 1995. In 1998, she applied to the National Aeronautics and Space Administration (NASA) astronaut program again. This time, Suni was accepted.

While Suni went through astronaut training, the first part of the International Space Station was launched, and her group of astronaut candidates became very involved with its development. Because Russia helps to operate the ISS, Suni and the other astronauts studied Russian. When the astronaut candidates were offered a chance to go to the city of Moscow to work on the Russian part of the ISS, Suni immediately volunteered. She helped read technical materials as they were translated from Russian to make sure they made sense in English. She also got to meet and work with the astronauts training at Star City, Russia's space center, to be the first crew to fly to the ISS. Suni watched in person as they launched into space from Kazakhstan on October 31, 2000.

After her time in Russia, Suni continued to work on different projects back in the US. In May 2002, she spent eight days living in Aquarius, an underwater station located off the coast of Florida. The underwater environment was meant to give astronauts an idea of what life in space might be like.

Soon, she would get a chance at the real thing.

The International Space Station

The International Space Station is the product of a partnership between the United States, Russia, Europe, Canada, and Japan. It was designed to conduct scientific research, to study the Earth's environment, and to aid future space exploration missions. The first part of the space station was launched into orbit in 1998. Additional parts were added on over time, and the ISS is now 239 feet wide and 356 feet long. It weighs 925,000 pounds. The ISS orbits about 250 miles

above Earth at a speed of 17,500 miles per hour.

Expedition 1, carrying the first human crew, arrived at the ISS in November 2000. Since then, over 280 astronauts from more than twenty countries have visited the station. They spend their time setting up and monitoring experiments, many of which focus on the effects of life in space on humans. They also try out new electronic equipment, like robots, and even test ways to grow their own fruit and vegetables!

The ISS is set to be retired in the 2030s. But there are already plans to build new space stations.

CHAPTER 2
Butch

Barry E. Wilmore was born on December 29, 1962, in Murfreesboro, Tennessee. He grew up in Mount Juliet, Tennessee, with his parents, Faye and Eugene, and his older brother, Jack. Barry's family was very involved with their church, and his Christian faith became an important part of his life.

After graduating from Mount Juliet High School in 1981, Barry attended Tennessee Tech University in nearby Cookeville. He planned to study electrical engineering, but he also had another goal. That was to play on the college's football team.

Barry (who wouldn't be called "Butch" until after he joined the navy) loved football. But he was five feet, nine inches tall and weighed 175 pounds, so he was considered small for the sport. He also described himself as "slow and weak." Still, he went to an open tryout and impressed the coaches enough to make the football team. He worked his way into a starting position for three games, but his season ended when he badly injured his knee. He had torn his ACL, part of the connective tissue that holds a knee joint together.

Barry in high school

It took a long time to recover from the knee injury, but Barry eventually was able to play football again. He grew two more inches, gained fifteen pounds, and became an important part of the team. Barry later said that managing his demanding engineering classes while training for football was the hardest thing he had ever done. But he felt that it gave him the experience he would need to meet other challenges in life.

As an engineering student, Barry had become intrigued by another challenge: how to land a plane on an aircraft carrier. He joined the navy and became a fleet naval officer, flying twenty-one combat missions from the carrier USS *Kennedy* during Operation Desert Storm in the early 1990s. He also completed missions for Operations Desert Shield and Southern Watch in the Middle East, and in Bosnia. During those missions, Barry made 663 carrier landings and had over eight thousand flight hours! He also picked up something else—the nickname "Butch," after the call sign he used as a pilot. A call sign is a short, easy-to-hear nickname that is used for radio communication while flying.

In 1992, Butch graduated from the US Navy Test Pilot School in Maryland. He carried out trials on different types of new aircraft and also became an instructor for future test pilots. In 1994, he earned two master's degrees: one in electrical engineering from Tennessee Tech and another in aviation systems from the University of Tennessee.

Butch loved to learn how things worked and was always looking for a new challenge. He decided that the next big challenge for him would be space. Butch applied for the astronaut training program twice but was turned down immediately both times. On his third try, he got an interview, but still didn't get in. He felt that he hadn't done well in the interview where he had to speak about himself. When he tried again in 2000, Butch spent hours practicing his interview skills with his wife, Deanna. Thousands of people applied, and this time, Butch was one of only seventeen accepted.

Butch was thirty-seven years old when he reported for training at Johnson Space Center in August 2000. Like all the other astronaut candidates, he had to learn how to fly the space shuttles that would be used to travel to the new International Space Station. They learned how to live in space and trained for space walks outside spacecraft.

The astronauts also practiced land and water survival training, just in case their spacecraft ever had to make an emergency landing in an unexpected place. Butch was sent with a crew to a forest outside of Moscow where they practiced setting up camps and surviving in freezing winter weather.

Just as Butch was starting his basic astronaut training, Suni was finishing hers. Neither knew it then, but someday they would be spending a lot of time together. A *lot* of time.

CHAPTER 3
First Flights

In 2003, Suni was named as a backup crew member for Expedition 14 to the ISS. Years can pass between the time a crew is named and the actual launch. That gives the astronauts time to keep training for life on the ISS and prepare for the work they will do on board.

Suni was thrilled when she was moved from a backup to a full member of the crew as a flight engineer. The first group of astronauts for Expedition 14 launched in September 2006. Then, on December 9, 2006, Suni's crew was ready to go. Suni had dreamed of going into space for so long that even as they waited to launch, it was hard to believe it was actually happening. But when they did finally set off in the NASA space shuttle *Discovery*, the whole crew burst into cheers. They were on their way.

The shuttle docked at the ISS on December 11, and the new crew went to work. Suni took part in experiments that tracked how the human body and materials like metals and plastics perform in space. She also participated in the regular work that is done daily to keep the space station running smoothly.

Like other astronauts, Suni had to work out for two hours a day. That's because there is no gravity in space or in the ISS. Gravity is the force that pulls people and objects downward. On Earth, people constantly use their muscles and bones to keep themselves upright and moving. That keeps their bones and muscles strong. But in space, the body doesn't have to do that kind of work. Bones and muscles become weak from lack of use. To stay strong, astronauts on the ISS need to exercise. That includes running. Astronauts wear a harness that is tied to a treadmill so they can run without floating away.

That was fine with Suni. She loved running. And in April 2007, she became the first person to run the Boston Marathon from space! (This time she had an official entry.)

Suni didn't just make history running inside the ISS. She also did her first space walks outside the space station. Astronauts usually do space walks to perform repairs or make changes to the outside of the space station. For space walks, astronauts wear a special space suit that supplies them with oxygen and keeps their temperature comfortable. During the walks, they are tethered to the station with strong cords. They have to move slowly and carefully and need to make sure the cords are always locked in place. To travel longer distances, they are moved by a giant robotic arm. The astronauts also wear an emergency jet pack in case they become separated from the station. By the time the expedition was done, Suni had recorded over twenty-nine hours of space walks, a record at the time for a female astronaut.

During her months on the ISS, Suni kept a blog and shared videos that allowed people to see the interesting work they were doing. One video showed astronaut Joan Higginbotham cutting Suni's long hair. She gave her hair to Locks of Love, a charity that uses donated hair to make wigs for children with cancer.

Suni loved her time in space. Although she was glad to return to her family and her husband, Michael Williams, in June, she looked forward to going back to the ISS.

Butch got his first chance to go into space a few years later. On November 16, 2009, he set off on STS-129, a short NASA mission to bring supplies to the ISS. Butch was the pilot of the space shuttle *Atlantis*. As the pilot, he had to make sure everything on the shuttle worked. Most importantly, he played a big part in docking the shuttle next to the ISS. Docking is very important because the shuttle has to be lined up and locked into place in order for astronauts to exit the shuttle and enter the ISS safely. The mission only lasted ten days, but it was a great chance for Butch to learn how the ISS worked.

On July 15, 2012, Suni departed for her next stay on the ISS as part of Expedition 32. ISS expeditions depart Earth with one number, but then when the previous crew leaves, the expedition gets a new number, and the senior member of that crew becomes commander of the expedition. As the senior member of the newly named Expedition 33, Suni became only the second woman to have commanded an ISS crew. That meant she was in charge of all the operations on the ISS and was responsible for the safety of the crew.

During this stay on the ISS, Suni worked on more experiments and got to take more space walks. Cargo ships brought them ice cream during the summer and candy at Halloween. Suni also completed a triathlon! She ran on the treadmill, biked on a stationary bike, and used a machine that simulated swimming strokes for the swim part of the race.

Suni returned to Earth on November 18, 2012. Once again, she had enjoyed her time in space. In fact, when asked during an interview on the ISS if she could imagine living up there for a whole year, she said yes.

On September 25, 2014, Butch set off on his next visit to the ISS. This time, he was there for a longer stay as commander of the crew. He also made his first space walk. Butch thought about how few people in the world get to walk in space and felt grateful for the opportunity.

Butch returned to Earth on March 11, 2015. He hoped he would get to go to the ISS again.

In 2024, he would get that chance. And so would Suni.

CHAPTER 4
Space Oddities

In 2011, NASA retired the space shuttles that had been used to fly to the ISS. NASA had been using the space shuttles since 1981. The shuttles looked like small jet planes and could make ground landings. They were supposed to be easy to reuse and maintain. But NASA decided that they were costing too much and weren't as reliable as they had hoped. NASA also wanted to put its time and energy into developing spacecraft that could fly to places that are farther away, like Mars. After 2011, astronauts flew to the ISS in Russian Soyuz capsules while privately owned businesses developed new spacecraft that could travel back and forth to the ISS. One was the SpaceX Dragon capsule, made by SpaceX. The other was being built by the aircraft company Boeing.

As NASA astronauts, Suni and Butch had been working with Boeing for several years on the development of their new Starliner. With their test pilot backgrounds, they brought a lot of experience to the process. They tested out the new capsule on land and helped Boeing understand what worked best for astronauts and what could make flights easier. It was fun to help create the new capsule, but they were looking forward to actually flying it.

They had a long wait, though. Various troubles with Boeing's Starliner caused delays, and the launch date kept being rescheduled. Meanwhile, SpaceX Dragons had begun to carry crew members to the ISS in 2020.

Finally, on June 5, 2024, Starliner launched with Suni and Butch on board. They were expected to arrive at the ISS, complete their work, and then return in eight days.

The launch went well, but as Starliner approached the ISS, problems began to pop up. Some of the reaction control system thrusters weren't working. These thrusters help steer the capsule. They play an important role in docking the capsule with the ISS. If they don't work, it is like trying to park a car with a broken steering wheel.

The capsule had been on automatic pilot mode, but Butch took control and piloted it manually for most of the rest of the journey. When they reached the space station, the capsule managed to dock safely. Butch and Suni boarded the ISS, where they were welcomed by the members of Expedition 71.

They soon discovered another problem, though. Starliner was leaking helium. Helium helps push fuel into the engines. If helium leaks out, the engines could fail.

The astronauts worked with NASA to

try to repair Starliner. But it was difficult to solve these problems in space. Their original departure date of June 14 came and went. On June 28, NASA decided that Suni and Butch would have to stay on the ISS longer while they worked on Starliner. They thought it could take a few more weeks or maybe even ninety days.

Butch and Suni joined in with the ISS crew's daily work. They helped with experiments focused on plant growth, 3D printing for certain metals, and the effects of microgravity on skin. Cargo capsules brought more supplies for the extra crew members—including more clothes for Suni and Butch, who had only packed for a trip that would have lasted around a week.

On August 18, Suni ran a seven-mile race from the ISS while her sister ran it at home in Massachusetts. The treadmill is located on a pathway through the space station. Other astronauts floated over Suni on their way to a different part of the station while she ran. It was just another day in space.

About a week later, on August 24, NASA made a big announcement. They didn't want to risk sending Butch and Suni back on the damaged Starliner. Instead, Starliner would return without them. The next crew was due to arrive in September. When that crew returned to Earth in February 2025, Suni and Butch would go with them.

By now, Butch and Suni's longer-than-expected stay on the ISS had become a big news story. People wondered why a capsule couldn't just pick them up and bring them home. Unfortunately, there aren't extra capsules just sitting around waiting like taxis. The missions are set years in advance. Changes can affect numerous other people. There are only a small number of seats on each capsule. If Suni and Butch took those seats on the next capsule leaving the ISS, other astronauts who had been there longer would have to wait. That wouldn't be fair.

And Butch and Suni were prepared for their stay. As test pilots, they always knew that plans could change. During an interview, Butch noted that they are trained to deal with the unexpected. And Suni admitted she was glad to have more time on the ISS. She called space her "happy place." There was always some work to do on the ISS—and it could be done upside down or sideways!

On September 6, Starliner flew back to Earth without a crew. It arrived safely.

During the summer and early fall, some astronauts left the ISS and others arrived. When the last members of Expedition 71 departed, Suni became commander of Expedition 72.

On September 29, SpaceX Crew-9, carrying astronaut Nick Hague and Russian cosmonaut Aleksandr Gorbunov, arrived. There were supposed to be four new crew members on that flight, but two had been removed in order to make room for Suni and Butch to travel back with them in 2025. That would be their ride home.

The Expedition 72 astronauts settled into their work. They spent their days doing experiments, making repairs, and, of course, working out.

But there also was time for fun. They stayed in contact with their families through video calls. The crew watched NFL and college football games together. Butch live streamed services from his home church and even made calls to church members who needed some extra prayers from space. They celebrated holidays with special dinners and decorations. Suni's birthday was also International Talk Like a Pirate Day, so she dressed as a pirate while they shared strawberry cake. At Christmas, the crew recorded a video posted by NASA. Candy canes floated by as they wished people on Earth a Merry Christmas.

Butch and Suni did many interviews about their extra-long stay on the ISS. People usually asked what they missed on Earth. Suni said she missed her husband and her dogs. Butch missed his wife, Deanna, and daughters Daryn, a college student, and Logan, a high school senior. They both said they missed fresh air, breezes, and the feeling of changing seasons.

In the meantime, though, they appreciated the opportunity to see Earth from 250 miles away. They could see the shimmers of the green northern and southern lights as they danced above the planet. As the continents rolled by, the astronauts tried to identify different locations. They tracked hurricanes as they whirled across land and sea. And each day, they got to watch the sun rise and set sixteen times. Suni never got tired of the view.

CHAPTER 5
A Long, Strange Trip

NASA had planned for the next crew, SpaceX Crew-10, to travel to the ISS in a new SpaceX Dragon capsule in February 2025. Once that crew was settled in, Crew-9, plus Suni and Butch, would return to Earth. But there were delays with the new capsule. In December, NASA decided that it wouldn't be ready to fly to the ISS until late March 2025.

People said that Butch and Suni were "stranded" and that they had been abandoned by NASA. But Suni and Butch never felt that way. They understood NASA's plans. They just kept doing their work. And at the end of January, Suni set a new record for spacewalking hours by a female astronaut. When a reporter asked Suni if she thought this might be her last stay at the ISS, Suni said that she hoped not. She loved being in space!

In February 2025, NASA announced that they would send Crew-10 to the ISS in a previously used SpaceX capsule instead of the new one as planned. Crew-9 could now return to Earth.

On March 16, Crew-10 arrived on the ISS. And at 1:05 a.m. on March 18, Suni Williams, Butch Wilmore, Nick Hague, and Aleksandr Gorbunov departed the ISS. Suni and Butch had spent a total of 286 days (that's nine months!) in space.

After they splashed down among the dolphins late in the afternoon of March 18, the astronauts were given a quick medical check and then were flown to Houston, Texas, where they underwent more medical tests. Then, at last, they were able to return to their homes.

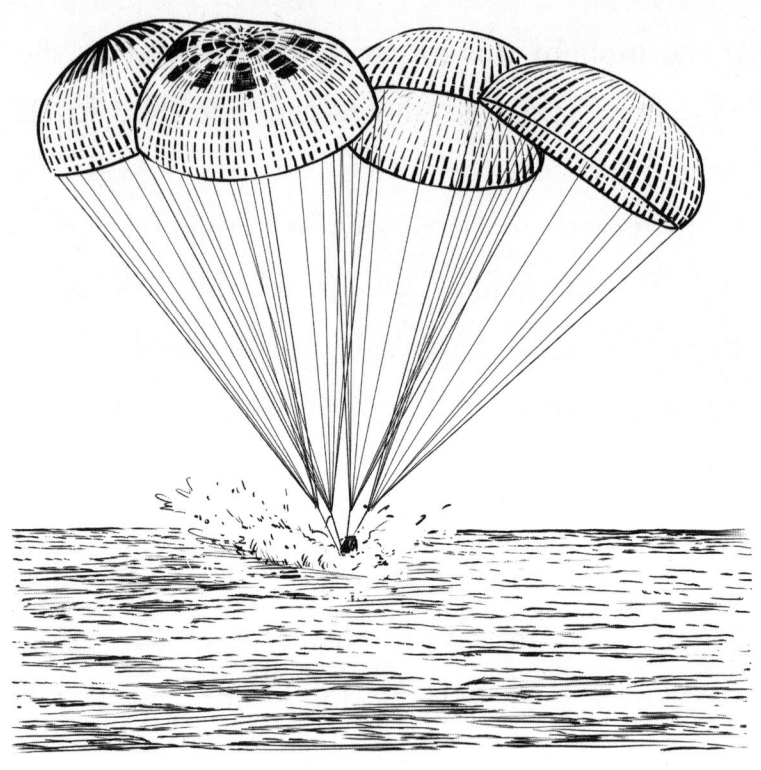

That didn't mean they could go back to their regular lives immediately. Astronauts who have been in space for a long time usually lose some strength. After floating around for months, they often have trouble with their balance. To recover, they return to the space center daily to undergo physical therapy and strength training.

Both Butch and Suni recovered well from their adventure. After only two weeks, Suni was able to complete a three-mile run!

In interviews, Suni and Butch said that they would continue to work on Boeing's Starliner. They thought it had a lot of potential and they would be happy to fly on it again. Butch said he wanted to go to the moon and Mars. Suni said she'd be there right beside him.

Butch and Suni said they were grateful that so many people had cared about them. And they were glad that their journey had brought so much attention to the ISS. In addition to all the scientific work being done there, the astronauts felt there were other important lessons to be learned. Life on the ISS showed how people from different cultures who spoke different languages could work together. Suni said that being in space encouraged people to problem solve and think outside the box. She thought it was a good reminder that life doesn't always go as planned, and that change isn't something to be scared of. Instead, it can be thought of as an opportunity.

Astronauts often experience something called the Overview Effect. It is a feeling they get from seeing the Earth in its entirety from so far away. Astronauts say it makes them feel more responsible for the planet and more connected to all humans.

Suni explained that being in space does change the way you think about the world. She said, "It's very peaceful up here. . . . It really is difficult for me to imagine people on Earth not getting along together. It's the one planet we have and we should all really be happy that we're there together, 'cause that's it. That's our place."

Suni Williams and Butch Wilmore set a great example of embracing life's challenges and overcoming setbacks. We're happy that they're a part of "our place" here on Earth.

Timeline of Suni and Butch's Lives

1962 — Barry "Butch" Wilmore is born on December 29 in Murfreesboro, Tennessee

1965 — Sunita "Suni" Pandya is born on September 19 in Euclid, Ohio

1985 — Barry graduates from Tennessee Tech

1987 — Suni graduates from the US Naval Academy

1992 — Barry graduates from the US Naval Test Pilot School

1993 — Suni graduates from the US Naval Test Pilot School

1998 — Suni is accepted into NASA's astronaut training program

2000 — Butch is accepted into NASA's astronaut training program

2006 — Suni flies to the ISS for the first time as part of Expedition 14

2009 — Butch flies to the ISS as the pilot of STS-129, a short cargo mission

2012 — Suni flies to the ISS as part of Expedition 32

2014 — Butch travels to the ISS as part of Expedition 41

2024 — Suni and Butch travel to the ISS in Boeing's Starliner

2025 — Suni and Butch return to Earth with SpaceX Crew-10 on March 18

Timeline of the World

1962 — The first Spider-Man comic book is released

1965 — The Gateway Arch is completed in St. Louis, Missouri

1970 — Rock music pioneers the Beatles release their last album, *Let It Be*

1976 — The United States celebrates its bicentennial

1980 — Mount Saint Helens, a volcano in Washington State, erupts

1985 — The wreckage of the RMS *Titanic* is found four hundred miles southeast of Newfoundland, Canada

1998 — The *Pokémon* animated series premieres in the United States

2005 — Hurricane Katrina devastates the US Gulf Coast

2010 — *Avatar* becomes the top-earning movie of all time

2013 — "Selfie" is the Oxford Dictionaries word of the year

2017 — A specific path across the United States from Oregon to South Carolina experiences a total solar eclipse

2019 — Scientists release the first images of a black hole

2022 — AI assistant ChatGPT is released to the general public

2024 — Baby pygmy hippo Moo Deng, born in Thailand, becomes an internet sensation

Bibliography

"2018 Theodore Roosevelt Award: Capt. Barry 'Butch' Wilmore."
NCAA. December 7, 2017. https://www.ncaa.org/
news/2017/12/7/2018-theodore-roosevelt-award-capt-barry-
butch-wilmore.aspx.

"Astronaut Friday: Sunita 'Suni' Williams." Space Center Houston.
March 1, 2019. https://spacecenter.org/astronaut-friday-
sunita-suni-williams/.

Barbaro, Michael. "NASA Astronauts to Return Home: Suni Williams
and Butch Wilmore's Unexpected 9-Month Space Odyssey."
Produced by New York Times Podcasts. *The Daily*. March
14, 2025. YouTube video, 14:22. https://www.youtube.com/
watch?v=q4zxDnOw5pg.

"Barry 'Butch' E. Wilmore." NASA. Updated March 18, 2025. https://
www.nasa.gov/people/barry-butch-e-wilmore/.

Dossett, Julian. "Why NASA's Starliner Mission Went from 10 Days to
9 Months: A Timeline." Space.com. Updated March 18, 2025.
https://www.space.com/space-exploration/international-
space-station/why-nasas-starliner-astronauts-spent-9-
months-in-space-on-a-10-day-mission-a-timeline.

Kumar, Aishwarya. "Inside NASA Astronaut Sunita Williams'
　　Journey through Space." *ESPN*. March 18, 2025. https://
　　www.espn.com/espn/story/_/id/44192592/astronaut-suni-
　　williams-starliner-runs-international-space-station-return-
　　earth.

"NASA Astronaut Suni Williams Talks with WBZ-TV Boston—Friday,
　　October 11, 2024." October 11, 2024. YouTube video, 24:40.
　　https://www.youtube.com/watch?v=I-YxHQbnGwA.

"NASA Astronaut Sunita L. Williams." NASA. Updated March 18,
　　2025. https://www.nasa.gov/humans-in-space/astronauts/
　　sunita-williams/.

Nawaz, Amna, and Azhar Merchant. "Astronauts Suni Williams
　　and Butch Wilmore on Their Longer than Expected Stay in
　　Space." *PBS News*. February 25, 2025. https://www.pbs.
　　org/newshour/show/astronauts-suni-williams-and-butch-
　　wilmore-on-their-longer-than-expected-stay-in-space.

Panjwani, Haya. "Behind the Story of the Return of Stuck NASA
　　Astronauts Butch Wilmore and Suni Williams." *Associated
　　Press*. Updated March 18, 2025. https://apnews.com/article/

stuck-astronauts-space-spacex-williams-wilmore-23138bc214
31771e91418d5cab40bbf4.

Williams, Sunita. "Suni Williams—June, 2009." Interview by Gary
Cohen. garycohenrunning.com. June 2009. http://www.
garycohenrunning.com/Interviews/Williams.aspx.

Williams, Sunita. Interview by Jennifer Ross-Nazzal. *International
Space Station Program Oral History Project*. NASA.
September 8, 2015. https://historycollection.jsc.nasa.gov/
JSCHistoryPortal/history/oral_histories/ISS/WilliamsSL/
WilliamsSL_9-8-15.htm.

Williams, Sunita, and Barry Wilmore. "Astronauts Waiting for
Months to Return Home Speak with Anderson Cooper about
Life in Space." Interview by Anderson Cooper. *Anderson
Cooper 360*. CNN. February 13, 2025. https://www.cnn.
com/2025/02/13/us/video/suni-williams-butch-wilmore-
boeing-starliner-astronauts-interview-ac-digvid.